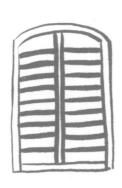

FROM MY WINDOW

Children at home during COVID-19

United Nations

ACKNOWLEDGEMENTS

From My Window was conceptualized, written, and illustrated by Xue Bai.

All queries on rights and licenses, including subsidiary rights, should be addressed to:
United Nations Publications
405 East 42nd Street, S-09FW001
New York, NY 10017
USA

Email: publications@un.org
Website: shop.un.org

ISBN: 978-92-1-101428-0
eISBN:978-92-1-005134-7
ePUB ISBN: 978-92-1-358354-8

INTRODUCTION

Written from the perspective of children who observe the world through their windows, this book for young readers looks at the lives of housebound children during the coronavirus pandemic. From Asia and Europe to North America, Latin America, and Africa, the book explores children's shared experience of life away from school and friends, wondering about the people in their lives and communities who are helping others and are in need of help. It shows children discovering what they can do to stay active and to support the people around them.

The stories in the book are inspired by true events and people. We hope that this beautifully-illustrated book will inspire children by showing them that we all have the same fears, and that we can overcome them by being creative and empathetic, and by staying positive and healthy. We will face other challenging situations in the future, and this book shows us that there are opportunities every day to love, learn, create, and connect, no matter the circumstances.

Look! There is no one on the street.

I don't go to school. And I can't go out to play with my friends. "Dad, what happened to us?"

Dad told me that there is a new type of virus that can get people sick. It can spread through the air when we are very close to each other. That's why we wash our hands a lot. And stay at home.

We are not the only family who stays at home. All our neighbors up and down the street stay at home, too.

But I guess the good part about staying inside is that I have plenty of time to read books.

I went through all my favourite books and wish so much that I could read together with my friends.

I have a brilliant idea!

Why not share my books with my friends online? We can see each other on our computer screens and can read the books together.

Mom has not been home for many days, and I miss her a lot.

Mom is a doctor and has been working so much because people in the hospital need her help.

When she does come home, I can't hug or kiss her. We have to keep our distance, so we can all stay healthy.

Even though we are far apart, we still find a way to connect and share love through music.

Every day at seven o'clock, we all open our windows and clap and sing to express our love and gratitude to the doctors and nurses and many others. People who are helping people. Just like my mom!

It's a very fun time of the day. For a moment, we just laugh and sing, knowing that we are not alone.

I know Mom can hear us.

Masks can protect us from the virus. But it is very sad to know that not every person in our neighbourhood has access to masks.

So, we started to make them ourselves!

I feel good when helping out. Life is not always easy. It's important that we look out for each other, and knowing that we'll ultimately get through this.

From my window, I see people standing in line for groceries, with all types of homemade masks.

They all stand in separate circles to keep a physical distance.

I haven't seen grandma for weeks. People say that senior citizens in our society face a higher risk of getting sick from the virus.

I want to make a card for grandma telling her how much I love her and miss her.

Since I can't get close to grandma I wave to her from outside her home. We talk to each other from opposite sides of the window, making funny faces, and laughing. It's so good to see her.

I left the artwork I made for her at her front door and hope she likes it.

Before leaving, I draw a flower on her window to cheer her up.

I Miss U

Baking is my favourite thing to do while staying in.

Now I am getting really, really busy, because my baked goods are very popular.

This is what I see from
my window.

Families who need food or
medicine will hang out a red
drape from their windows so
that people with good hearts
know that they need help.

People who can help and
have something to give put a
green drape to signal that we
are here to help.

I put my baked goods in paper
bags and leave them outside
their front doors.

The world is waking up.

After months, my friend and I can finally go out and meet.

Today is the day!

After a long winter, spring always comes.
Never stop believing. Together we can
get through anything.

WHAT CAN YOU DO?

JOIN THE SDG BOOK CLUB

The #SDGBookClub aims to use books as a tool to encourage children ages 6-12 to interact with the principles of the Sustainable Development Goals (SDGs) through a curated reading list of books from around the world related to each of the 17 SDGs in all six official UN languages—Arabic, Chinese, English, French, Russian, and Spanish.

Join today!
Share your view from your window
Share your story and meet new friends

www.un.org/sustainabledevelopment/sdg-book-club-archive/

READ THIS BOOK

My Hero is You: How Kids Can Fight COVID-19!
A new fictional book developed by and for
children aims to help families understand and
cope with COVID-19. With the help of a fantasy
creature, Ario, this book explains how children
can protect themselves, their families and
friends from coronavirus and how to manage
difficult emotions when confronted with a new
and rapidly changing reality. Available in six
languages (Arabic, Chinese, English, French,
Russian, and Spanish). To download a free copy,
visit www.unicef.org/coronavirus/my-hero-you.

PARENTS, TALK WITH YOUR CHILD

How to Talk to Your Child about Coronavirus Disease 2019 (COVID-19)
UNICEF offers parents guidance on how to speak with their children
about the coronavirus disease. To see the eight (8) tips to help comfort
and protect children, visit www.unicef.org/coronavirus/how-talk-your-
child-about-coronavirus-covid-19.

THE UN IS DOING ITS PART

 United Nations

The **United Nations (UN)** has been working to reduce COVID-19's negative impact on children, who are facing new health risks, disruptions to their education and increased exposure to domestic violence and hunger.
For more information, visit www.un.org.

 World Health Organization

The **World Health Organization (WHO)** is leading and coordinating the global effort against COVID-19, supporting countries to prevent, detect, and respond to the pandemic.
For more information, visit www.who.int.

 unicef

The **United Nations Children's Fund (UNICEF)** partners with COVID-19 front-line responders to keep children healthy and learning, protected from sickness and violence, no matter who they are or where they live.
For more information, visit www.unicef.org.